# My Spring
# of Hope

## Hellen Frost

A Passion for Learning
Kent Enterprise House, The Links, Herne Bay, Kent.
CT6 7GQ United Kingdom
www.apassionforlearning.co.uk

Copyright © 2013 Hellen Frost

ISBN  9781849143899

Cover design: Hellen Frost
Illustrations and photography: Hellen and Steve Frost
Printed by Lightning Source International, UK

First Edition 2013

*For my husband Steve,*

*In you I have found the missing half that has now made me whole.*

# Contents

# Acknowledgements

Thank you Steve, my life has changed so much for the better since God sat you in front of me in church. You have been patient, kind and encouraged me to continue with writing this when life seemed so busy I thought would never be able to put aside time to finish writing this book.

Thank you, Fluffy, for sticking with me in true friendship. I hope I have been a help more than a hindrance to you! I am so proud of the steps you have made over the last year and long for the day when you see yourself as we see you. You are beautiful, loving, kind and very precious to me.

Thank you Tracy for becoming such a treasured friend, for teaching me to listen and know God's love and for feeding me chocolate and reading thrillers in the van on our long journeys!

Thank you, Marilyn, for being my friend that understands my excitement about gadgets and leads and the importance of packing them first when we go away..... It's been such a healing and growing experience being part of your ministry team. I never thought I would be helping with prayer ministry, seeing and sharing pictures as well as being a driver/sound engineer. I love the way you set me new challenges every time, even when you decide not to let me know what song you want a backing track for......

Thank you again to my family at the Beacon Church who have continued to love and support me. Especially to John and Jo, Steve and Jenny, Emma, Kay and those who have been very patient and tolerant of me in my cell group. Keep sharing and showing the love of God to those that walk through the doors of Beacon as you did to me, I love you all.

Thank you Lizzie, you have been a precious friend and I pray you will always feel Gods healing love.

Thank you to all the fellow Christian's I have continued to meet over the last year all over the country as I have travelled to churches and Christian centres with Marilyn, Tracy, Saffie and Goldie. It's been such a blessing to hear feedback of how people have been touched, healing that's occurred and new love that's been understood. Marilyn's team have taught me so much about how God can use us to minister in so many ways and have nurtured and encouraged me.

And the most important of all, thank you God for being my Daddy, my life has changed completely because of your true unconditional love. Your grace has set me free. Please continue to teach me to walk in Your light every day.

# Foreword

As I read 'My Spring of Hope' I felt moved to tears. The poems, anecdotes, insights and pictures that Hellen shares with us are so real, coming as they do from her heart and deepest experiences of her relationship with her Father God. They spring out of the reality of her life with all its pain, joy, hope, loss, beauty, grief, fear and love. As you read you enter into her journey, likened here to the seasons of a year, and somehow, that journey becomes yours too and you find that through the simple line of a poem, or a word, picture or phrase that your own feelings, longings and experiences are given flesh and you feel the stirrings of tears, hope or laughter: deep reaching unto the deep of our own hearts.

It is a jewel of a book and a wonderful sequel to Hellen's first book, 'His Blood Not Mine'. You can read great chunks of it at once like indulging in a rich feast, or enjoy a dainty titbit! You can start at the beginning and work steadily through or dip here and there. However you go about it, I can guarantee you will be fed, moved and uplifted as you read. Enjoy it and be blessed.

I have personally come away feeling inspired to live my life fully for God, not holding back because of any past hurts or fears, but to live each day with the expectancy that my Father may give me insight through something as insignificant as tea spilling over into the saucer, just as Hellen experiences and expects.

I have known Hellen for a few years now and I respect and honour her so much for walking this journey with such perseverance even through the many hard times she has faced. It has been and still is such a joy and privilege to share some of that journey with her as she works with Marilyn and I in MBM. Thank you, Hellen for being you. You have had a huge impact, not just on me but on all who are encouraged and helped by you sharing your testimony and poems at our events and I know this book will be a real source of joy and a channel of God's Father love to many.
*Tracy Williamson*

In the last few years, Hellen has experienced some deep and wonderful changes in her life. She has met with God her Father, her spirit has come alive, and He has awakened her heart to all the beauty of Creation and His love. As she looks at the ordinary things of life, God speaks to her, and she is able to write down her feelings and her spiritual awareness. Her thoughts and poems are insightful and inspiring. She often shares them at our conferences and people are deeply moved, not just because of the words said, but because they can see she is speaking from her heart. Her passion for Jesus is contagious and also very challenging.

Hellen, it's a privilege to work with you and an even greater joy and privilege to know you.
*Marilyn Baker*

# Introduction

It's been an amazing time since I published 'His Blood Not Mine'. I have been astounded and humbled by the responses from people who have read the poems and the variety of situations in which they have been used. It's been such a blessing to know that times of such struggles for me are now bearing fruit and helping others who are struggling in their own lives.

Life is a continuing journey of ups and downs, I have faced new battles but now I know that I have my Father God on my side and that however desperate I may feel, if I turn back to Him I can face those battles head on.

*If God is for us, who can be against us?*
*Romans 8 v31*

I have continued to move forward. I love being a teacher and it's amazing that my tutoring business is going from strength to strength, although I am still learning lessons in putting aside time for myself, my husband and time to be still with God. I do not hear Him when I am so busy, when the noises of life drown out His voice in my heart. But in those times I have given to myself, the times I have been away with Marilyn Baker and Tracy Williamson, both when serving on the MBM team or just spending time with friends, times whilst running in the woods and walking in the countryside, those are the times when I clearly hear Him, as its when I listen, really listen, to what He is saying.

The new poems that are in this book have come from a variety of situations, from times of happiness and times of sadness, from simple everyday objects that have just stood out and because I noticed them, stopped and asked God "what are you saying to me through this?" It's amazing how He has touched my heart so often in this way.

I have had the privilege of praying for people through prayer ministry and anointing as part of the MBM team, it has once again been a learning curve but working alongside other members of the team, I have begun to sense what God is saying and how He is guiding me during those times. At first I think I was trying too hard, but when I stopped trying and just let Him work through me, I have had some amazing and beautiful pictures come to me that I have been able to share with those I have been praying for. I realised that it is not me doing the ministry or the anointing but that it is God working through me, He is in charge, in control and I just have to be a willing servant.

Sharing these poems throughout the year and through this book gives me such strength and hope that the struggles I have been and am going through will be used to enable healing in others.

My life has continued to change, through meeting a lovely Christian man at my church, Steve. I never expected to meet my soul-mate, I had trusted God, in that I knew if there was to be someone He would provide the situation for us to meet, but I have to be honest I never really expected it would happen, and if it did I wasn't sure if I could ever feel safe with a man again. But God knew, He knew me, His timing was perfect. Only a few weeks before getting to know Steve I was tested about how I really felt about being female, if I really was comfortable in my body. It was a difficult time but lead to deep healing and laying down things that were still hurting me at the foot of the cross. God knew I was now ready to meet somebody that would see me as I really am and not who I thought I was from the past. There have already been challenges, from others who have judged, from those with their own hurts, but each one has strengthened the relationship between Steve and I and my faith and trust in God. Loving another person so deeply in this way is amazing and I thank God every day for everything I have been given. I could never have loved in this way before God taught me about true unconditional love. Steve and I are now married and just starting on our journey as husband and wife, discovering the exciting plans God has in store for us together. I have no idea of what He's got in store (which is probably a good thing...) but I am willing and trust Him to lead me on His path.

I hope once again that those who read this book will be blessed in the same way I have been as I have written the poems in it, this is not for me. If just one person finds their way to start on their path to healing then it will have been worth every second and every tear of sadness and of joy.

# Part One

*Spring*

# My Spring of Hope

*At a session with Tony Horsfall on Lectio Divina, he read Isaiah 35 v1-2. We had to see what stood out to us and the word that shone brightly for me was 'crocus'. I felt that God was saying to me that "this is your spring". I was blooming and rejoicing but that it also meant I had to absorb as much as I could now before the summer, autumn and winter when there may not be as much nutrients around me. This will mean I can continue to bloom, grow strong roots and shine for Him all year round.*

A crocus is a sign of spring,
Of life and colour after a bleak winter,
The start of the blooms about to spring
    forth in a rush of growth.
A new cycle of life beginning for the year
    ahead.
As I listen quietly I hear Your voice
    Lord,
Whispering "My child you are that
    crocus now,
This is your spring after a long bleak
    winter,
A time for rapid growth,
Soaking in My love for the coming
    seasons.
Strengthening your roots so you can
    stand tall with your head held high
    for Me."
So I will bloom brightly with a new joy
    in my heart,
A flower of Your hope.

For there are now seasons ahead,
Dread of the future replaced by a trust
   in Your plans for me,
Of the hope I now have.
This is my spring of hope.


*The desert and the parched land will be*
*glad; the wilderness will rejoice and*
*blossom.  Like the crocus, it will burst*
*into bloom; it will rejoice greatly and*
*shout for joy. NIV*
*Isaiah 35 v1-2*

# A Tiny Seed

*Some of the weeds in my garden have such beautiful flowers I have left them growing. Weeds grow even when the land is barren. I had a picture of a sprouting seed in a landscape ravaged by a flood, a fragile new life emerging that some might think is not worth much but it is what God has chosen to create, a unique beautiful flower of God. I was reborn as a fragile new seed in the barrenness of my life ravaged by rape, I didn't feel beautiful, but to God I am, and as I have grown I have come to know many other beautiful flowers, reborn through His love.*

The tiny seeds shell cracked open and a
    small shoot emerged,
There was no light underground, but the
    gentle    warmth    of    spring    had
    awakened it and a new life begun.

When the shoot reached the soils surface
    the sunlight was almost too bright,
But it bravely unfurled its first leaves
    and started to grow.

The landscape was barren and rubble
    strewn around,
The flood had destroyed and swept away
    all previous life.

The precious seedling grew higher
    tentatively at first,
But as its roots began to reach out and
    build a firm foundation,

The fragile plant gained strength and
grew taller day by day.

In a garden it might have been a weed
by any other name,
Pulled up and removed unwanted so the
chosen plants could grow,
But on this barren ground there was no
one to pull it out,
The weed was protected and with hope a
bud began to form.

The flower grew inside, curled up
tightly, all alone,
But when the bud split open, its petals
unfurled and a beautiful flower was
seen.

And the flower was alone no longer,
For other weeds had grown too, the land
desolate no more,
Beautiful bold colours spread out as far
as the eye could see,
Life was blossoming here from those
who had been protected,
Plants called weeds before were not
weeds here in Gods new garden.

The flower held its head up high proud
to be chosen by it's Father God,
And inside tiny seeds began to form,
Ready to be sown when the time was
right.
Will you be that flower of God?

# Love, Faith, Hope

*When asked what had changed when I was healed from my mental illness and self-harm, I replied that one of the biggest things was hope. I now had hope. To know God has plans for my future, that He will always love and care for me, helped me believe I actually had a future. Before it was hard to think about the next hour, let alone the next year. Sometimes I had to manage by just focusing on the next breath. In fact a precious friend told me "Just breathe, anything else is optional!" But now I have hope. I thought hard about where that hope came from and I knew it was God's love. Love that gave me faith, faith in God and in myself. If I had faith in God I must believe in His promises of what He plans for me, bringing hope in my heart for the future. Love brings faith, giving hope.*

Love came first and found me in the
    beginning,
It reached in and touched my broken
    heart,
Spreading healing warmth from within.
Love brought me back to life,
Love protects me, holds me,
My Father's true love.

Faith then spread throughout my heart
    and soul,
Changing the way I think, live and feel,
I may not see but I know He's there.
Faith brought me assurance,
Faith was a precious gift,
My Father's true faith.

Hope was the true path to end all my
    suffering,
A reason to forgive, to love, to be healed,
I have such certainty in that hope.
Hope brought with it a future,
Hope gave me new life,
My Father's true Hope.


*And now these three remain: faith, hope
and love. But the greatest of these is love.*
*1 Corinthians 13 v 13*

# An Overflowing Cup of Love

*During a Beacon service, Fred shared a picture to do with holding your cup up to the Lord so He could fill it and share it with you. It may have been to do with a Bible verse but I didn't know what, it was just the picture that stood out to me, a cup filled by God's love but not just full, so full it was running over. I looked up online to see if there were any Bible verses and I came across the song "Drinking from my saucer" by Michael Combs which seemed a fitting ending – not missing out on a single drop!*

Is your cup empty?
Half empty or even half full?
Not even a full cup is enough for me!
Not even brimming full!!
'Cos my cup is an overflowing cup of love!

Overflowing with blessing,
Overflowing with more than I ever asked or thought,
Overflowing with His love and mercy.

Why I do not know,
I have not earned or deserved this,
I'm just an ordinary person.
But it is extraordinary that I'm alive!
Saved by grace, by love.
From a pit so deep, so dark not even the sun could penetrate.

But God could reach His hand down to
    me,
Scoop me into His palm,
Lift me up into the light,
While protecting me from its brightness,
And proudly showing me for all too see.

So you see it's amazing my cup is that
    full,
But then who takes a full cup to a well
    to drink?
Only an empty cup can be filled with
    Christ's goodness,
The wine of His love brimmed and
    running over,
But none must be wasted
So......
I'm drinking from my saucer 'cos my cup
    is overflowing!

# I Wake and I Hear the Birds Sing

*During a period of not sleeping to well I was awake before dawn. It was still dark but I could hear the birds singing already! When the light came it was grey outside but the birds still sang with joy. As it was coming up to Easter I was looking at the story in the Bible and I hadn't realised that when the angel rolled back the tombstone Jesus had already risen and left the tomb! It had to be rolled back so that people would see and believe it. I also learnt that it became dark when He was crucified and it reminded me of the total solar eclipse I saw in 1999, I remembered reading that the birds would stop singing during the eclipse, as they would think it was night and I asked myself did the birds stop singing when Jesus was crucified and what would they start to sing again afterwards?*

I wake and I hear the birds singing,
It's early and still dark but they know
   the dawn is coming.
But even the birds were silent that day,
The day Jesus died on the cross.
The sky was dark as even the sun bowed
   in grief.
The birds could no longer sing a song of
   joy-
Would dawn ever come again?
But after two days of sadness and
   despair,
The angel came and rolled back the
   tombstone,
So all could see Christ had risen!

Hope reignited the world,
The birds began to sing once again,
A new song, a song never sung before,
For History was now changed forever,
A new dawn had begun.
I am now certain my dawn will come
  every day.
Jesus died and rose again to pay for this
  certainty, this life I now have,
This day, this precious day when Jesus
  saved me,
Born again to an eternal life.

So as I wake early and hear the birds
  sing,
Before the dawn they are certain is
  coming,
My heart sings with joy as I am certain
  He is coming,
And I will be with Him.

# Creation

*Having believed in and taught evolution before becoming a Christian, I took a leap of faith at first believing in creation as written in Genesis. As a scientist I soon wanted to discover more, and as I did I found that the evidence backed up creation. Yes, there may be no 'hard' evidence for God but in my heart I know He exists and therefore created everything including me. To have been designed for a purpose before the start of time is so amazing. I often found myself thinking I don't really matter, that it would make no difference if I was not here. But if God thought I was important enough to be part of His world, and I believe in Him, I must believe in this too.*

I am a creation,
Not an accident,
Not a chance.
I believe that I was created by God,
A God so powerful, so awesome, above everything.
I believe too that I was created deliberately.
Each cell chosen and crafted by His hand.
He made me like no other,
He made you this way too.
Each one of us is special,
Unique.
With a purpose only you can fulfil,
A plan designed only for you,
A plan designed only for me.

He created me,
Not once but twice,
I was created when I was born,
And I was created anew when reborn in
the water of the Holy Spirit.

I worship and praise You my Creator,
my God and my Father.
I kneel down humbled before the One
who loves me,
The One who loves you,
Yes you.

*In the beginning God created the
heavens and the earth....
So God created man in his own image, in
the image of God he created him; male
and female he created them.*
*Genesis 1 v1 and 27 ESV*

*Therefore, if anyone is in Christ, he is a
new creation. The old has passed away;
behold, the new has come.*
*2 Corinthians 5 v17 ESV*

# Early in the Morning

*Driving through Tonbridge early in the morning in the van on the way to an event it was so quiet. No traffic only the odd delivery and dustbin van. But preparations were going on to start the day, making it ready for others. It made me wonder what I am preparing for my day ahead, what will I do for God today?*

It's early in the morning,
As I drive through the streets.
The world is just awakening,
Activity just beginning.
The only people out are those preparing
    the day ahead for the rest of us.
The road sweepers, bakers, delivery
    men.
People we don't always see,
There in the background,
But they are those who make the world
    how we expect it to be.

God prepares the day ahead for me.
I feel His presence so strongly this
    morning,
He has been preparing me all night as I
    sleep,
Developing His covenant within me.

As I wake He calls me to use my faith to
  do His work.
I wake into a world I didn't make.
I wake into a salvation I did not earn.
God's grace came first,
And greets me every morning.

Will I use this day to enjoy, share and
  develop the works He started last
  night?
Will I rise to walk on grace and faith?
For I have been built by His quiet gentle
  strength,
God gave me the power to do what
  pleases Him not me.
It's His story,
Not my story,
His story.

# God Loves You

*A dear friend struggling with living but yet trying so very hard to keep breathing couldn't see how God could still love her when she didn't feel she was very loving towards her friends. I know that God loves us however we are. He may not like what we sometimes do but it doesn't stop Him loving us. I wrote this for my friend as I just wanted her to know how much God loved her no matter what.*

God loves you when you're happy,
God loves you when you're sad.
God loves you when you shout out loud,
God loves you when you're mad.

God loves you when you're nice to
    friends,
God loves you when you're not.
God loves you when you're quiet and
    calm,
And when you've lost the plot.

God loves you when you have a smile,
God loves you when you cry.
God loves you when you cannot breathe,
And when you really try.

God loves you when you're grumpy,
God loves you when you're blue.
God loves you when you hurt inside,
And don't know what to do.

God loves you in the sunshine,
God loves you in the rain.
God loves you when you still do it
 wrong,
Over and over again.

God loves you all the time,
No matter what you do.
God loves you just the same,
Just as I love you too.

*God is love*
*1 John 4 v16 NIV*

# God Loves You (Outstanding!)

*After I read my 'God Loves You' poem at church, John said it would make a good children's song and suggested to that to Steve Dunn, who wrote this song. We have now learnt it at church and it has gone down really well at family zone. It was so precious to hear it the first time and I know that so many people need to understand that God loves them and that He is the best Father you could ever want or have.*

> God loves you when you are happy (I'm over the moon!)
> God loves you when you are sad (Now I'm feeling blue...)
> God loves you when you're relaxing (I'm taking a break!)
> God loves you when you go mad (I'm a total fruitcake!)
>
> Chorus
> He loves you in the sunshine; He loves you in the rain.
> He thinks you're great no matter what,
> 'Cos Christ the Son has paid for all our shame!
> He is outstanding, unchanging, in control and so amazing;
> The best Father a child could ever dream.
> He is outstanding, unchanging, in control and so amazing;
> The best Father a child could ever dream... in your wildest dreams.

God loves you when you are happy (I'm
  pleased as punch!)
God loves you when you are sad (Now
  I'm down in the dumps...)
God loves you when you're relaxing (I'm
  loosening up!)
God loves you when you go mad (Now
  I'm off my nut!)

# Some Days the Light Shines Brightly

*I was really struck by God being a lamp for my feet, lighting the path ahead. I thought of camping with my head torch, it really only shows the next footstep, I cannot see far ahead, I don't always know what's coming. God sometimes only lights up enough to take a footstep, I don't know what's ahead but He does. I have to trust in Him to guide me. I can be confident in each step I take whether I see the path ahead or not.*

Some days the light shines brightly and
    the whole path ahead can be seen.
Other times the darkness is almost
    overwhelming,
I fear I will lose my way,
I can't see the path ahead,
Uncertain as to what the future holds.

But there is now always a small light
    there,
Just the glow of a lamp,
Enough to light only my feet.
Yet it means I can see the footstep I
    have to take,
Just one at a time.

To do this I must trust.
Trust that God knows the path ahead,
That He will guide me,
That He will not let me stumble.
He will light every step I have to take,
His mercies are there new every
    morning,
His love will never cease.

*Your word is a lamp to my feet and a
light to my path.*
*Psalm 119 v105 ESV*

# Part Two

*Summer*

# The Beauty of God's Creation

*I wrote this while at the Black Forest. As we drove around it was just too green and beautiful. Someone at home had said I would get bored of the trees but that was just not possible – God's creation here was amazing! As a science teacher I find I am expected to teach 'the theory of evolution'. I agree totally with evolution within a species but now I have gone from accepting evolution between species without question to totally believing creation as written in Genesis. As a scientist I wanted to look at all the evidence and nothing I have seen makes me question this belief but if I am too accept this I must also accept myself as God's beautiful creation too. I find it extremely hard to think of myself as beautiful, my past makes me feel ugly and ashamed but that is not how He sees me.*

> I look around me and I see such beauty.
> The greens of fields and the forests,
> The pinks of the flowers,
> The blue of the sky,
> The clearness of the rushing water.

> I now know this did not happen by chance collisions of atoms in a primordial soup.
> Formed slowly over millions of years.
> I used to believe this but now I cannot.

I cannot look at this beauty and not
know that each leaf, flower and
creature was lovingly designed by a
creator.
The creator that designed you and I to
be unique,
Each with our own fingerprints that
were formed in our mother's womb.

I look around at such beauty and am
stunned and amazed by God and
what He has done.
Sometimes I forget this when I look at
myself.
To think that I am unique and that God
made me as His beautiful creation.
It can be hard some days to say I am
beautiful, when all I see in the mirror
is the ugliness of who I was.

But that is not who I am now,
Reborn as God's precious child,
Cleansed and full of the radiance of His
light.
Light that I must let shine from me for
all too see,
To guide them too as part of God's
beautiful creation.

So I remember as I look around me at
the beauty of the mountains, fields
and forests,
That I am part of this beauty too.
God's beautiful, amazing creation.

*For you created my inmost being; you knit me together in my mother's womb. I praise you because I am fearfully and wonderfully made; your works are wonderful, I know that full well.*
*Psalm 139 v13-14 NIV*

# The Sound of the Peace of Our King

*Arriving at a retreat at Haus Barnabus in the Black Forest, Germany I was exhausted. It had been a very busy time in the pre-exam period and I was very blessed to have to been given the opportunity to go away by Marilyn. When we arrived, the hosts Len and Phyl said they wanted us to feel as if this was our home while we were there, to relax and take time from our busy lives. The first two days there I think I must have slept most of the time! It was obviously what I needed to do. While out I was struck by the sounds that I felt were peaceful and started to record them on my phone and when I wanted to give something back to Len and Phyl I wrote them in this poem.*
*http://haus-barnabas.blogspot.com/2011_05_01_archive.html*

I feel this peace in this house,
It fills my soul from the inside out,
Permeating my whole being.
This is the perfect peace of our King.

I feel this peace when I walk down this
   path,
I hear the peace of the burbling stream,
The sing song of the birds in the forest,
The chirping of the crickets in the
   rustling meadow grass.
This is the perfect peace of our King.

I feel this peace when my mind is stayed
upon Him.
I can lean right into Him, my rock of
trust.
I can be confident of the hope I have in
His plans for me,
As I lie down in this house and listen to
the perfect and constant peace of the
Lord our King.

*You will guard him and keep him in*
*perfect and constant peace whose*
*mind [both it's inclination and it's*
*character] is stayed on You, because*
*he commits himself to You, leans on*
*You, and hopes confidently in You.*
*So trust in the Lord (commit yourself*
*to Him, lean on Him, hope confidently*
*in Him) forever; for the Lord God is an*
*everlasting Rock [the Rock of Ages].*
*Isaiah 26 v3-4 AMP*

# Rains of Joy

*When I was teaching in Peru we used to do a residential fieldtrip to the Tambopata rainforest. The school was in Lima on the west coast where it doesn't rain, just a miserable sea fog in the winter months. However, on the second evening in the jungle the heavens opened with a real tropical downpour, it was around bedtime but the students came running out and were dancing in the rain, screaming with joy. For they had never, ever experienced rain. I started to think of how I felt when I first felt Gods rain fall on me, the joy when I felt His love and wondered how it must be not to have felt this rain, the rain of His love.*

It's hard to imagine having never felt
    the rain,
To have lived in a dry and barren land,
The dust swirling, plants withered, soil
    cracked beneath your feet.
For then one day to have the sky open
    and the rain stream down to earth,
To run outside with your arms held high
    in the pouring rain,
To shout with joy as drops of rain soak
    you to the skin.

I want it to rain!
I want the heavens to open!
The rain to pour down!
To be so thirsty for God's rain,
The rain of His Spirit.
To be bathed by a river so full,
Washed away by the waves flooding over
    its banks.

Lord let Your rain pour down,
Let me feel the joy like never before.
Soak me as if for the first time ever,
As I hold my arms up to You.

Have you ever felt God's rain?
Truly felt His rain?
Is being soaked a dread or a joy?
Do you run out into His rain with your
     arms held high?
Soaked with God's Spirit to your skin,
Letting His rain pour over you.

# As I sit at His Feet

*During the first evening worship at Church on the Farm
with our local New Frontiers churches I had a picture of
children sitting at Jesus's feet listening to Him tell them
stories and His robes were so long they flowed over the
floor so that the children were sitting on them. As I
looked I realised one of the children was me, I can be a
child when I am with Him and just experience a father's
love with my simple faith.*

His robes reach out beneath me,
I feel safe, warm and secure.
His voice speaks softly but with
authority and assurance.
He tells stories to the children who sit at
His feet,
They listen gazing up, knowing His love.

For I am one of those children,
Sitting on Jesus' robes,
Listening to His voice,
Knowing His love.

Jesus so awesome, so powerful,
Yet so tender and gentle.
Teaching of His love so that we may too
love like Him.
I sit at His feet and gaze up into those
beautiful eyes,
Eyes full of mercy,
Eyes full of love,
Eyes that look down at so many but also
just at me.

I am His child,
His Father is my Father.
He loves me as His Father loves Him.

Lord let me radiate that love,
Bathe those lost and hurting,
Draw them close so they may too sit at
  your feet,
To look, listen and feel that amazing
  heavenly Father love.
As they sit with me at Your feet.

# Fire Burn in Me

*One of the speakers at Church on the Farm said that he so wanted "Fire to fall down" on him. When I went to bed that phrase stuck with me and I wrote down my thoughts by the light of my iPod in my tent. I thought the words I wrote were for me but the next morning during the service, the same speaker said he wanted the church leaders to come to the front for prayer, to receive God's fire. Some of his words were the exact ones I had written so I knew in my heart that my words were for John, the lead elder at the Beacon Church. I was hesitant about giving someone my words for them but it was so on my heart that I sat and wrote the poem out there and then and gave it to him. The following week John read part of the poem at a prayer evening and said it was so appropriate for how he had been feeling, the weariness in his soul, but how he so wanted to feel that fire falling down on him again. He said that the church should encourage me in receiving prophetic words, wow I thought! I had never expected to hear the word prophetic about me. Could God speak through me?*

Fire burn in me,
Ignite my soul,
Burn through right to my core,
Leave behind the ashes that are purely
    You.
Burn from me all that is not righteous,
All that is not for Your glory,
All that is not in the spirit of Your love.

Fire fall down,
Fire fall down,
Fire fall down on me.

You are the air we breathe,
You are the fuel we eat,
You are the spark that ignites all
    flames.

You are all I want,
You are all I need,
You are everything.

I may feel tired and weary,
Wonder who am I to receive this fire?
But a smouldering wick He does not
    snuff out,
He gently blows His living love on the
    ember,
Reigniting the flame of passion,
Feeding it until the fire is burning high
    and bright,
So that every man on earth can see its
    glory.
Fire burn in me,
Fire burn in me,
Fire never, ever die down,
Fire just fall down and burn in me.

# The Prince of Peace

*Tracy often reads from her Kindle to Marilyn and I when we are travelling to events in the van. The first book she read was 'Heaven is for real' by Todd Burpo. It's an amazing book about his son Colton, who was seriously ill and saw Jesus in heaven during an operation to save his life. Colton's experience came out bit by bit to his parents until they realised he must have really met Jesus! Todd searched for ages with Colton to find an image of Jesus which looked just as he had seen him, but to no avail until they found painting by eight year old Akian Kramarik, of the Jesus that she had seen in a vision of heaven called 'The Prince of Peace'. Colton was always saying the problem with the other pictures was: "And His eyes, oh dad, His eyes are so pretty!" When his dad showed him the picture and asked what was "wrong with this one, Colton?" he went very silent and then said, "Dad, that one's right." The painting was included in the back of the book and when I saw it, I was touched deeply inside; there really was something about His eyes that looked right into me. I searched in the Bible to see where the name 'Prince of Peace' came from and found the verse in Isaiah 9, I also came across a song by Michael W. Smith called 'You are Holy', also known as 'Prince of Peace', and the chorus finishes with the line "You're my Prince of Peace and I will live my life for You". That's what I want to do.*

> A Prince that stands strong and tall
>   against my foes,
> A Prince that holds me gently in His
>   arms.
> And His eyes,
> His eyes are so beautiful.

I gaze into these eyes
And I feel a warmth but yet a longing
    inside.
I want to see those eyes for real every
    day,
Those beautiful, beautiful eyes.

He will meet me in heaven when I
    arrive,
Holding out those strong hands,
Taking mine in His,
Holding them tight.
As I stand in front of Him,
The Prince of Peace,
And see the love in those beautiful,
    beautiful eyes.
He is the Prince of Peace
And I will live my life for Him.

*"And his name shall be called Wonderful
Counsellor, Mighty God, Everlasting
Father, Prince of Peace."*
*Isaiah 9 v6*

© A. Kramarik 2003

# Dads

*At the Outlook Trust conference I really felt some of the older guests needed encouragement about the role they could still play in their church. I know how important it was for me to have an older couple as a role model for a Christian family relationship and to be my 'God' mum and dad. Trying to understand that God was my dad was so hard for me at first. My experience of a dad was not what I wanted him to be. But through building father relationships at church I learnt that God was different. His love was so much more. The role model that 'dads' in church can play to help people to understand God's love is so, so important and this poem came from that and I shared it later that day and hope it encouraged those there.*

> Dads can be short,
> And dads can be tall.
> Dads can have a great big belly,
> Or when turned sideways be nothing at
>     all.
>
> Dads can have scratchy beards,
> And dads can be bald.
> Dads can be young,
> Or be ever so old.
>
> Dads can be strong,
> And dads can be gentle.
> Dads can be quiet and calm,
> Or can act completely mental.

Dads words can be kind,
Or they can cut like a knife.
Dads can make you happy,
Or make you want to end your life.

Dads can be full of love,
Or dads can destroy.
Dads can give the bestest hug,
Or be distant and without joy.

Dads will you be like our God of love?
Dads will you model our Dad from
above?

Dads will you show what a family can
be?
Dads you can't change the past
But dads you could be all you could be.

# The King is in the House!

*Going back to Brunel for the second year I knew of the tradition Ron had of getting everyone to declare in the mornings that "The King is in the house!" It was amazing to think that Jesus was right there with us. But then I thought of the passage in the Bible where Jesus will only enter to those who open the door themselves He knocks. It is I who has to invite Him into my house; He will not just come in, even though He could, until I ask.*

> The King is in the House!
> But will I let Him in?
> Into the inner sanctuary of my heart?
> The core of my soul?
> "But He is the King!" I hear you say,
> "He can go anywhere He wants!"
> But He won't,
> He waits for me to unlock the stone door
>     to my heart.
>
> But when I do it's amazing,
> My heart of stone starts to soften,
> My mouth starts to try to form a smile.
> It   feels   strange   at   first,   even
>     uncomfortable,
> To open my heart so wide,
> But I feel His strength, His joy, His love,
> Fill me from the inside out.

For my King is the King of glory.
Strong and triumphant in the battle of
    my past,
The heart pain to be banished from His
    kingdom forever,
To be replaced by love, by peace, by joy,
I wear the smile more and more now,
I can even laugh, can love, can hug.

How precious, how amazing.
My King is in my house.

*Behold, I stand at the door and knock. If
anyone hears my voice and opens the
door, I will come in to him and eat with
him, and he with me.*
*Revelation 3 v20 ESV*

# I Belong to You

*At Brunel I had a deep feeling that for someone there the idea of change was so hard and frightening. I remember this feeling when my life was starting to change. I was becoming independent, studying at uni and thinking about if I would be going back to work. Sometimes I would feel that I was moving forward so fast that I was lost as I didn't know my new surroundings. Change is hard, I had to let go of being ill, take responsibility for being healthy and make wise decisions and choices for myself. Gradually reducing the amount of support I had from others was a slow but necessary process. I worried that friends would leave me if I wasn't so needy, were they only with me because I needed help? Would I be abandoned? I had to remember that God would never abandon me, He would always be there. If I needed help or just a hug, I only had to ask for I now and always would belong to Him.*

> I belong to you,
> What does this mean?
> It means comfort
> But    also    means    handing    over
>     everything,
> Everything that is mine is yours,
> Everything that is good,
> But also everything that is bad.
>
> Handing over my problems is not easy,
> It means not being in control anymore.
> Change is hard, it is a challenge,
> To wake up the next day,
> And know I have changed.

But being uncertain of the future,
Of the unfamiliar feelings,
Not knowing the path ahead.

But Father I trust in you.
I belong to you.
I am yours.
I love you.

# I Feel the Sand Under my Feet

*While staying at St Rhadagunds on the Isle of Wight, I was amazed by the beauty; it was autumn but so warm and sunny. I paddled in the sea with Marilyn, we thought it was a nice sandy beach but it turned out that the sand was quite rough, almost like grit and not very comfortable at all! But later in the day I could feel the smoothness of the soles of my feet, how the rough sand had removed my roughness. I have so many rough edges, I even feel spiky at times; why would anyone want to love me?*

I feel the sand under my feet,
Wearing off the dead layers of skin.
I feel smooth soles.

Waves in turn smooth the rocks,
Into pebbles,
Into grit,
Into sand.

Once all rough edges are smoothed,
The resulting sand is wonderful.
But it takes time.
It doesn't happen overnight.
It's the slow repetitive effect of the waves.

God's love is like that to me.
Slow, gentle and repetitive.
Over and over again,
He tells me He loves me.

The roughness is smoothed,
The spikiness worn down,
The protective layers built up from
years of hurt,
Ground steadily away.

I can build castles with sand.
He can build lives with me.
The tide washes the sand away.
The lives He builds remain for
eternity.

# A Living Well

*Staying alive day after day sometimes felt hard, I started and finished the day tired and weary. But my life force now came from God, to be refreshed I only had to drink of His Holy Spirit. But this is an active and not a passive process. To be cleansed inside I have to seek and let His Spirit in. However long the road is, there will always be a well to drink from.*

*Therefore the well was called Beer-Lahai-Roi*
*[a well to the Living One who sees me]*
*Genesis 16 v14 (AMP)*

A living well,
Full of anointing healing power.
A well to guard your heart.
This well is the spring of life,
Water full of the Holy Spirit.
The Lord says to me,
"Let Me in,
Let Me right in,
To bathe those areas of your heart only
    you know about,
So secret, so hard to enter".
Oh heavenly Father let me say yes Lord
    when I hear Your voice,
Let me allow Your living Spirit to wash
    through my soul.
Cleanse me,
Renew me with the water that can only
    come from Your well.
I open myself to you Lord.
Live within me O Holy One.

# Dreaming

*We were coming to the end of a retreat, and a friend was always so worried that all she had gained during that time would leave her as soon as she went back to her life outside this haven. That night I dreamt we were all leaving but that I had written a short poem for that friend. I wanted her to know that if she truly received the gifts she had been given that week they would not leave her and neither would God. When I woke I remembered vividly the exact words of the brief poem I had written. A poem from a dream.*

> The precious gifts that have filled the
>     depths of my heart,
> Will not leave me when I leave here,
> For they have been impregnated deep
>     within me by God's love.

# Part Three

## *Autumn*

# The Prison

*During a trip to Swansea for the Torch anniversary with Marilyn and Tracy we were booked to lead the Sunday service at Swansea prison. This terrified me, I looked up the prison on the internet and saw it was a high security men's prison. What type of crime would they have committed I was asking myself? Would any of them have raped? As a rape victim I didn't know how I could be in the same place as someone who was a rapist. We arrived at the high grey stone wall of the prison and I lost count of how many locked gates and doors we went through to reach the chapel and the noises of the keys and buzzers really struck me. The experience of meeting the men, however, was life changing. I saw how they listened and showed genuine compassion when Tracy and I both shared our testimony and they sang the hymns with Marilyn and I was so touched when at the end a number of them came to shake our hands. Outside the prison many had no family, security or prospects for the future. Only God can give them hope. A high security prison is not the only type of prison though, the sounds I heard that day triggered sounds from long, long ago. But I have escaped from that prison! God gave me family, security and prospects for the future. I am willingly in a prison now, a prisoner of hope.*

> Keys jangling,
> Buzzers sounding,
> Gates clanging,
> Locks clicking.
> These are the sounds of a prison.

Gentle weeping,
An angry voice rising,
A fist thumping,
A door slamming.
These are the sounds of a prison.

A waiting silence,
Approaching footsteps,
A handle moving,
A belt undoing.
These are the sounds of a prison.

A joyful laugh,
A bleeping text,
Music playing,
A bird singing.
These are the sounds of my prison!

A prison?
Yes I am a prisoner,
No longer imprisoned in the waterless
    pit,
But in a stronghold of security and
    prosperity.
For I am now a prisoner of hope!

Defended and protected by the Lord my
    God,
As precious as the jewels of a crown,
    shining gloriously.
For His beauty and goodness are so
    great, so powerful.

So a prisoner I will willingly be,
A prisoner of the hope I now have of
     eternal life,
The prosperity of love in my heart.

Joy, love, mercy, tenderness.
These are the Walls of my prison.

*As for you also, because of the blood of*
*my covenant with you, I will set your*
*prisoners free from the waterless pit.*
*Return to your stronghold, O*
*prisoners of hope; today I declare that*
*I will restore to you double.*
*Zechariah 9 v11-12 ESV*

# Alone

*It had been a difficult and long evening. I was feeling that others didn't care, had not taken into account my feelings and how tired I was. I went to bed and cried. I felt so alone. Yes I was surrounded by team and other guests but I lay feeling rejected and abandoned. As my tears fell I suddenly knew my Father was right there beside me, I was not alone and never would be. If I felt like this, how must some of the guests who were on their own and in the middle of tough times feel? Rather than feeling "nobody loves me" perhaps I should start letting others know that I loved them just as God loves me.*

I feel alone in a building full of people.
I want a hug but cannot ask.
Away from others I shed silent tears,
But as I cry I feel arms around my
    shoulders,
My Dad whispers in my ear:
"I am here, hand it all to me my child"
"Rest and sleep in my arms tonight so
    that tomorrow you can go into the
    world with your head held high and
    be with others again"
As I snuggle into His arms I know I am
    so blessed to be so loved.
If I feel lonely with all this love, others
    must too,
And maybe tomorrow I can be the one to
    give them the hug they cannot ask
    for, but long for.
Because the truth is with God as my
    father,
I am never, ever alone.

# A Soldier Surrenders

*At church Fred shared a word about how he had seen
people with their arms raised in worship during the
previous song. He said that when he was in the armed
forces, arms raised meant surrender. What does it
mean to surrender to God? Why would I do that during
worship?*

The soldier advanced slowly,
Head bowed down in defeat,
Arms raised high in surrender.
He knew it was the only way his life
    could be saved.
The battle could not be won.

I worship with my arms raised high,
Does that mean I am surrendering?
Yes, total and complete surrender,
Nothing less will save my life.
But my head is held high,
My battle has been won,
Freedom in God's love.

So here I am to worship and offer myself
    to God,
Lifting up my heart and hands, to
    heaven,
To the Almighty One,
The only One.

*I will praise you as long as I live, and in
your name I will lift up my hands.*
*Psalm 63 v4 NIV*

# Taken

*While shopping I had my wallet stolen. It had everything in it, cards, driving licence and all those little notes that I had tucked in the back. I was very upset and worried that it would be used to steal my identity, but after quite a few phone calls most things were sorted and I set up an ID monitoring system with my bank. But I still felt miserable, almost violated. I was away the next day with Marilyn and Tracy at a church weekend and went to bed exhausted but unable to sleep. Whilst lying awake I realised that what had been taken was material. There was no way anyone could take away who I was. God had changed me, moulded me into the person I am now. No one on this Earth can change that.*

It was taken.
By whom I do not know,
Just taken.
And yet when left with nothing,
I suddenly find I have everything!
I may have no ID,
But I am still ME.
I may have no money,
But then who can buy love?
These material things can be replaced,
But I cannot.

I lie here remembering the person that I
    was,
Seeing the person I am now.
Are they the same I wonder?
All those things that were taken so long
    ago.

Love, trust, innocence, childhood.
All the things I have now been given.
Life, hope, love, family, forgiveness.

So now I have nothing,
I know I truly have everything.
Everything I really need.
He gave me what cannot be taken.
God gave me back me.

# A Tear Falls Down From Heaven

*Listening to someone sharing over lunch at Pilgrim Hall who felt he had let God down so that was why God was not talking to him, I felt that God was crying out to him and felt every moment of his pain and just wanted to take him in His arms and hold him tenderly. The same day a dear friend at home was struggling hugely with suicidal feelings and was texting me while I was in the evening session. I went to bed feeling sad and helpless that I was not there for her and could do nothing to make her better, but then I realised just being there is what she needed, the rest I take to God.*

A tear falls down from heaven,
One of many that has come,
You lift your head and ask,
"Why are you sad what is it I have
   done?"

Oh my wonderful child I forgive you,
For what you think you do,
It's for your sadness that I cry,
These precious tears for you.

My soul is heavy from the weight,
Of your sinking heart,
I want to hold your hand,
If your clenched fists will only part.

It's not what you have done to me,
But what others did to you,
You feel there is no hope for life,
But that really isn't true.

You think I am not speaking,
But it's you that does not hear,
O precious one please seek me,
You'll see I'm always near.

You cannot find the way yourself,
Only I can guide your path,
To the future that awaits you,
Far from that awful past.

Oh dear child you think I don't know,
What it is your feeling now,
But every pain inside hurts me,
Though you'll never know quite how.

So lift your face to heaven,
And feel my tears from above,
Each one is wept for you,
With my unfailing love.

Unclench your hand,
And hold mine tight,
For alone you just cannot
    stand and fight.
Oh my child feel my love
Throughout your wounded soul,
New hope can only spring from,
The love for you I hold.

So have faith and let me lead you forth,
To this life I've planned for you,
Just pray and I will listen
As you'll find I always do.

# The Battle

*We sang two songs during Sunday worship at the Beacon Church whose words struck me: 'There is power in the name of Jesus' by Noel Richards and 'Be thou my vision'. Both spoke of a battle but that the power of Jesus would bring the victory. I was in a battle, but who with? And this battle I was losing fast....*

> *No one is like you, Lord; you are great,*
> *and your name is mighty in power.*
> *Jeremiah 10 v6 NIV*

The battle was raging swift and strong,
The fight seemed it would never end.
When I saw the enemy,
I also saw there part of me.
Some days I almost made progress,
But most I did not.
A steady retreat happening day by day,
Defeat looming, inevitable.

But then I surrendered.
Not to the other side,
But to God.
Full and total surrender.
The battle tide turned,
I could now fight back,
New weapons were at my disposal.

The enemy fought bitter and hard,
But my armour now repelled his shots.
I was still under attack,
But I was now fighting back.

For there is no other name higher than
    the name of Jesus,
The one name with the power of a
    mighty sword.

And with this sword I now stand and
    fight.
For my God is my armour,
My breastplate, my might.
I fire bullets of glory,
Shoot flaming shells of passion.
Enemies fall and enemies are crushed,
Demons flee.
And once a captive, now I'm freed.
For my sin is defeated,
I will never retreat again.

I'm marching forward in strength,
Strength Gained only from God.
In surrender I gave my all,
In surrender I gained so, so much more.

*Stand therefore, having fastened on the
belt of truth, and having put on the
breastplate of righteousness, and, as
shoes for your feet, having put on the
readiness given by the gospel of peace. In
all circumstances take up the shield of
faith, with which you can extinguish all
the flaming darts of the evil one; and
take the helmet of salvation, and the
sword of the Spirit, which is the word of
God,*
*Ephesians 6 v14-17 ESV*

# Scars

*Watching the end of an episode of the TV series 'Criminal Minds' about a team of FBI profilers, one of the agents asked if the victim would ever recover from the awful things that had happened. The other agent replied:*

*"Scars remind us where we have been.*
*They don't have to dictate where we are*
*going. "*

*I am covered with scars after years of self-harm, they are slowly fading but they are a visible daily reminder of what has happened. I can even remember when some particular injuries were made. But it's my past, not my future.*

*I've had a dream that there was a burning white fire with someone the other side. It was Jesus and He said to me "Put your arms into the flames" and even though I was afraid I did and the scars disappeared from my arms. I have no idea if this will ever happen in this life time. Meanwhile God is using my scars in His ministry to speak to people about self-harm and to give people that have harmed themselves the courage to speak to me. It's breaking down barriers.*

My scars tell a story,
Each one a memory, picture or emotion.
They are present both inside and out.
People can only see the outer scars,
Probably it's the inner scars I see more.

But a scar does mean I have healed.
Yes I was once hurt, injured,
Then new tissue formed over the wound.
The scar started red and angry,
But now gradually fades over time.

My body healed the outer scars,
Only God can heal the inner ones.
They may still take time to fade,
They will probably always be there,
But they are not me.

They do not lead me forwards,
They will not hold me back.
My scars tell of my past wounds,
My present healing,
But not of the future God's planned for
    me.

# The Wall

*My school teachers used to speak of the wall I had built up in front of me. If I was already building my protective wall back then, how high must it have been when things were at their worst? When life was unbearable and I could only cope by hurting myself, totally isolated behind that wall. There was surely nothing that could break it down now? I was wrong, I didn't know about God....*

The wall.
Tall and mighty,
Impenetrable.
But where did it come from?
Who built it?

I did.
Brick by brick.
For 34 years.
Every brick a brick of hurt,
Of pain,
Of harsh words,
Of broken trust,
Of lost love.

The wall grew slowly but surely,
It grew so tall in height.
A wall of complete protection.
Until no one could see in,
But neither could I see out.

I was shut in for so many long years,
Until I too started to crumble behind my
	wall.

But then I heard a voice through the
    wall,
A voice of love.
I took down some of the highest layers,
I peered over the top.
There were people, looking,
Searching for a door to reach me.
The voice still spoke love,
So I removed bricks lower down,
A hand reached through to me and took
    mine gently,
I took down more bricks slowly,
    hesitantly,
Until I could fit through.

It was hard to leave the safety of my
    wall,
But I've never turned back.
For I've found family,
Love,
Community,
Trust.

I can depend on others,
They can depend on me.
I love and am loved.

And who was the voice?
It was God my Father.
He knew I was lost there behind my
    wall,
He saved me.
He can save you.

# Who Am I to Do This for You?

*As part of the MBM team at a retreat in Green Pastures I was privileged to be able to take part in prayer ministry for the first time. I also had a girl come to visit me who was self-harming and wanted to meet me as I have come through this experience. I had such doubts in the middle of this, who was I to be working in this way for God? What did I know? What could I offer? I felt Him say that all I needed to do was be willing to let Him work through me, I did not need to heal people, He would do that. My past would help me lead others to Him.*

Who am I to do this for You?
Who am I to serve?
I have been broken,
Worn down,
Damaged.
How can I work for you after this?
What strength do I have left?
What do I do?

But You are a great God!
You are a mighty God!
You are an awesome God!

For it is Your truth,
Your restoration within me so powerful.
I can now radiate your light and love.

So what should I do Father?
His voice whispers to me,
"Nothing My child,
Nothing except to listen to Me.

Listen to My voice,
Listen to My heart of love".

If I pray in Your name,
I pray with authority,
With power.
I may have been broken,
But I am not broken now.
I have been built back entirely by You
   God,
I would not be here but for You.

Your heart is my heart,
Yes I know and understand
Suffering,
Grief,
Pain,
But so do You.
Much more than I ever can.

# I Listen as the Rain Beats Down

*With Marilyn and Tracy at Green Pastures it rained and rained. We sat listening to it pour down and we could hear it beating on the conservatory roof. When I walked Pennie down the Chine towards the beach the leaves and debris had been washed down into the stream blocking the flow at first but then everything became washed clean as the rain continued to beat down. If the flow is strong enough nothing will be left behind!*

I listen as the rain beats down.
I watch as it streams into the channel.
Debris is washed away,
Dead leaves, soil, rubbish.
As it washes down,
Some debris gets caught on the rocks in
    the stream,
Other debris then sticks to it,
Threatening to block the channel.

But the rain continues to pour down,
It rushes and roars down the channel,
Removing it all and washing it into the
    sea,
The brick walls guiding the torrent,
Protecting the banks,
Stopping it overflowing.
The stream is now clear and fresh,
The surrounding paths washed clean.

His spirit pours through me,
Washing all debris away.
I must not cling to it,
But let it pour from me.
No rocks will trap the past within me,
He will protect me,
He will guide me through this,
Even when it hurts so much inside.
He will heal that pain.

I am cleansed.
I am free.
I am loved.
I am Gods precious child.

# Part Four

*Winter*

# The Raging Storm

*In worship at church we sang 'In Christ alone, my hope is found' by Stuart Townsend. I had sung it many times before but that morning the words struck me powerfully. Life was better now that I was beginning to heal, but that didn't mean that it would never be difficult. Storms will still sometimes rage around me but now I am safe and secure on Him, my rock. All I need to do is hold on tight.*

The storm rages around me,
But also within my heart.
The winds blow and deafen Your voice,
The waves beat and batter and steer me
off Your course.

But I can stand firm on this solid
ground,
In Christ alone my hope will be found.
He will calm the winds,
He will smooth the waves.
If only I stop struggling against them,
To be still, trust and rest above the
storm.
Held in God'
s arms,
Supported by His love alone.

Storms will always come,
But struggling or resting firm is my
choice.
So I choose His rock of love.
I live for Him and with Him.
I rest still above the storm.

# Christmas Day

*I woke on Christmas day feeling unusually happy.
Christmas has been a hard time of year but this day I
seemed to feel truly glad.  I was going to church for the
first time on Christmas day, which was special, and it
really felt like a celebration of Christ's birthday! Things
can and do change, bad made into good, tears of
sadness into tears of joy.*

Christmas was a time of sadness, of
grief and unhappy painful time with
family.
But this morning I wake full of joy,
Because Christmas now is a time of
celebration, of peace, of happy times
with new family.
So I willingly come to praise and
worship the day You came to earth,
Born to die for me.
The most amazing gift I could I ever
wish for.
The most precious gift I have ever
received.
This is the day Christ was born,
Christ's day.
Praise the lord!

*And she gave birth to her firstborn Son
and she wrapped Him in swaddling
cloths and laid Him in a manger.*
*Luke 2 v7 ESV*

# The Dawn Sky Glows

*I had really been struck by a song by Nathan Tasker called 'Love is the Compass'. The picture of a compass just stuck in my mind, always there to guide me back home to God. I woke up early to a beautiful sunrise, the whole sky red announcing the arrival of a new day. Each of these days can be different, some happy, some sad, some peaceful, some a struggle with difficult emotions but I can always follow my compass home.*

The dawn sky glows red,
As the sun rises in the east,
Bringing a new day that the Lord has made.

The evening sky is ablaze with glory,
The sun sets in the west,
Bringing the day to a close, resting for tomorrow.

Joy may come from the north,
Suffering from the south,
Hope rising in the east,
Peace setting in the west.

But Your compass Father,
Will always guide me home.
Your love is always there to pull me back to You,
No matter how lost I feel I am.

Whether I walk to the north, east, south or west,
Your love brings me home.

# Feathers of Ice

*It was New Year at a house party in Harnhill, the water on the van windscreen had frozen into beautiful feathery leaves and it was as if God had turned something simple into something beautiful to remind me what He has done with me. I find it so hard to think I am beautiful in God's eyes, I feel what has happened in the past inside will show as ugliness on the outside. But that's not how God sees me.*

The morning sun reflected off the glass,
Sparkling with such joy.
Looking closer I could see the ice,
Not normal frost but beautiful ice crystals.
Interwoven leaves of ice,
Each intricately formed from tiny feathers,
Swirling and joining together intimately.
How could something that was so beautiful, form from something so simple as water?
Beauty from such plainness.

It was a gentle reminder from God,
Of the transformation within me.
I am ordinary, simple, plain.
But now I have Christ within me,
His radiance shines from me.
Making me beautiful in His eyes,
Intricately woven and created by His
hands.
His Sonlight will sparkle off me for all to
see and believe in Him.

# White as Snow

*Snow fell overnight, I walked to church crunching through the fresh snow and quite a few others ventured out too! Eileen shared during worship how the snow soon became dirty and was no longer beautiful but that we were white as snow always as said in Isaiah. I looked up the verse and knew that I too had become 'white as snow'.*

The snow's freshly fallen,
A beautiful glimmering white layer,
Untouched by human hand,
Blanketing all that lies beneath.

But soon it is trodden in,
Driven over,
The whiteness fading,
Grey creeping in.
And soon the snow is no longer
    beautiful,
I start to wish it would just melt away.

But the opposite has happened to me.
I started off dirty, stained.
I wished I could just melt away,
Leave this life I could not bear.

But Jesus came to change all that,
His blanket of love took away all that
    stained me,
Until I too was white as snow,
As pure as Jesus himself,
Washed clean by His blood.

And though I may gain new stains every
    day,
As I tread through life and it treads on
    me,
His blood continues to daily wash me
    clean with forgiveness,
Until I am once again
White as snow.

*"Come now, let us reason together", says
the Lord. "Though your sins are like
scarlet, they shall be as white as snow;
though they are red like crimson, they
shall become like wool."*
*Isaiah 1 v18 ESV*

# Cascades of Ice

*In Germany with Marilyn and Hilary we were driving back to our lovely hosts Helmut and Theres in Suggental. I saw a waterfall on the rocky cliff by the road. Because of the freezing temperatures most of the fall was ice but there was still water flowing through the centre, where it had not frozen because of the continual movement. It was beautiful and the image remained in my head. It made me think of the way the Holy Spirit needs to continually flow through us, melting our core no matter how cold it is spiritually outside.*

> The ice cascades down the rocky cliff,
> Cold, hard and white.
> Frozen in time.
> But inside the water gushes,
> A seemingly living force,
> Kept alive solely by movement,
> The continual flow of water falling from
> above.
> A slower trickle would have frozen long
> ago,
> But this waterfall was fed from a strong
> stream,
> Falling, forcing its way through the
> tunnel of ice.
>
> Sometimes my faith may begin to freeze,
> I find myself in a cold inhospitable
> wasteland,
> A land where the Holy Spirit does not
> flow.

Those around me blocking its life force
from above.
But if my faith is strong and steadfast,
If I actively seek out God,
Allow the Holy Spirit to flow freely
through me,
I will never freeze to the core.
God's living love will always melt my
heart,
Always keep me soft inside.

For there is no force stronger than this
one.
The force that will be with me until this
body dies.
For if I let Gods Spirit pour through me,
The outside world may seem frozen,
But inside I will still flow.
For I am truly alive.

## Two Layers of Tea

*Sitting at the breakfast table the sun was streaming through the window. I had just poured my tea into a glass cup and the sun showed that adding the milk had formed two distinct layers in the tea. It made me think of the things that form a boundary between God and me, when my life is led by me or the things around me and not God. To make the tea properly it needed a stir, I need to stir my faith to break through that boundary, to fully lean on God.*

Two layers formed in the tea,
The milk stayed below,
Almost pure tea on top,
A distinct boundary between.

My relationship with God can become
    layered,
It is sometimes easy to separate
    everyday life
From my walk with God.
Not relying on Him
When I try to solve my daily problems.
Being independent,
Not God dependant.

So I need a spoon,
To stir up my faith.
Remove the boundary between myself
    and God,
So that I rely on Him,
Turn to Him at every point in my day,
Lean on Him in times of weakness,
Rejoice with Him in times of joy.

No separation,
No boundary,
Joined as one.


*Do you not know? Have you not heard?
The Lord is the everlasting God, the
Creator of the ends of the earth. He will
not grow tired or weary, and his
understanding no one can fathom. He
gives strength to the weary and increases
the power of the weak. Even youths grow
tired and weary, and young men stumble
and fall; but those who hope in the Lord
will renew their strength. They will soar
on wings like eagles; they will run and
not grow weary, they will walk and not
be faint.
Isaiah 40 v28-31*

# Thumbprints

*It was another sunny morning sitting by the window at breakfast, enjoying my toast and honey before a beautiful day in Germany. There was a spoon in the honey pot, the sun was shining on it and I could clearly see my thumbprint from where I had just used it on the end of the handle. It wouldn't last long though, soon to be wiped off by someone else or by washing. I saw a picture of God's thumbprint on my Heart, identifying me as His, a print that would never fade for I am His forever.*

My Thumbprint shined on the spoon,
Glistening in the sun.
It's beautiful in it's uniqueness,
One of a kind,
Identifying only me.

But it will not last long.
It will soon be smudged, wiped or
washed off,
So it's clean the next time it's used.

God's fingerprint on me is permanent.
It can never be removed.
It's Unique to me,
My Birthmark,
Imprinted onto my heart
When I was reborn into His family,
Shining Forever.

# A Living Light

*A beautiful sunny morning in the midst of winter, the rays of the sun pouring warmth into my heart, bringing me out of the greyness of winter, filling me with unexpected new life. Those rays of light felt as though they were from God, His living light pouring into me, giving me so much. The first line of the poem came to me, the things I get from God every day, from His living light.*

Light, warmth, love, strength, peace.
My God, my Father shines down on me.

His warmth fills my heart and renews
   my soul,
I am strong in His strength,
I love through His love,
I fight for peace as I feel His peace.

As I learn to step out in my faith,
To walk this new life daily,
I will sing songs of praise,
For I am His and He is mine.

Light, warmth, love, strength, peace.
My God, my Father shines down on me.

*"I am the light of the world. Whoever follows me will not walk in darkness, but will have the light of life."*
*John 8 v12 ESV*

# The Sun Sets Slowly

*Driving towards Nottingham in the MBM van with Tracy and Goldie the sun was just setting. The sky went from ordinary to glorious as the sun slowly fell below the horizon. Everything became silhouetted by the amazing reds of the sky behind. It looked to me at that moment like a royal carpet stretching towards heaven, towards my King. A sunset fit for not just any king, but my King. The King.*

The sun sets slowly before me,
A glorious red filling the sky.
Trees are silhouetted on the horizon,
Lights blinking on one by one,
The day drawing to a close.

As the sun sets lower the red intensifies,
A thin band between heaven and earth,
Like a royal carpet for a king.
A sense of expectation fills the air;
Who is this king I wait for?

He is the mighty King of heaven and of
    earth,
King above all other kings.
More powerful than any earthly ruler,
Now, in the past or in times to come.

But my King needs no red carpet to
    enter my heart,
For He is so gentle in His power.
As I ask Him to reign in my life,
To be part of His kingdom.

And who is this King of all kings?
He is Jesus Christ.
My King.
My Ruler.
My Saviour.

So I gaze in wonder and awe at the
    majestic sky,
Thinking of Him,
Because this is a sunset fit for my King.

# New Snow Falls

*A thin layer of new snow, just a couple of centimetres had fallen. But it was enough to cover up the leftover dirty slush and ice from the week before. Looking out it was almost as if that dirty layer did not exist underneath, but it was still there just covered. It struck me how different my 'snow white' layer was, not covering up the stains but completely washing me clean, no dirt remaining.*

A new layer of snow has fallen,
Not much but enough to cover the
    remaining snow,
Left over from the week before.
The ice, slush and dirt of the week,
Covered as if they were not there,
Hiding underneath.

But the love of Jesus that blankets me is
    not like that.
It did not just cover up the stains I had,
So they could not be seen.
The love of Jesus completely washed
    those sins away.
They are not hiding underneath,
They are banished for eternity.

The new layer of Christ is the only layer
    that covers me.
A Holy white layer,
Clothing me with God's love.

# Part Five

*A New Season*

# Joy

*I am a terrible morning person.... For the first hour I wander about, get easily side-tracked and can be very grumpy! But this particular Sunday morning I woke with a feeling of joy in my heart, joy I never used to have, a joy I now know that comes from God.*

Today I feel joyful,
I awoke with joy my heart!
But not every day is like that,
I can feel tired and weary,
From when I get up to when I go to bed.
The day passes in a blur of exhaustion.

Those days I do not feel joyful,
Those days I forget the reason I am
    here.
That I am only here because of You,
That You restored my broken life,
Renewed my heart and soul.
So that I can feel joy,
Experience love,
Live in hope.

Joy is here for a reason:
Jesus died to give me a new life.
Through joy I am alive.

# The Woman

*At Offa House with Marilyn I was really struggling. I had been on medication to stop my menstrual cycle while I was suffering from mental ill health as I had found that my self-harm was more frequent and severe when I was coming up to my period, a severe form of PMT greatly magnifying my depression. I had stopped having these injections a year before but my cycle had not resumed and I didn't know if it ever would as I'd had the treatment for so long. But on the way to the retreat my first period started and it really sent me into turmoil. Part of me was relieved that it was ok and I could still have a family in the future; the other half of me was terrified. I felt like a victim again. I was a woman when I was raped and abused; did this make me that person again? I suffered from vivid flashback nightmares for two nights and felt terrible. Talking to a good friend on the team I realised I had still not handed over everything, I was still clutching past pain and blame in my heart. So at the end of the retreat I went down to the wooden cross at the bottom of the garden and laid those things down, asked forgiveness for not wanting to be the woman God created me to be. I then accepted myself as Hellen the woman again, a princess of The King.*

A small child learning the differences
    between man and woman too early,
But not understanding why.
A young girl wondering what would
    change,
Seeing others around her becoming
    different.
A teenager looking at her friends that
    are happy to be with boys,

Why didn't they know what she knew?
A young woman knowing there was
    something wrong with her,
That she was damaged goods forever.
A woman in tears ashamed that she no
    longer wanted to be as she was
    created,
That she was ugly both inside and out.

But God still loved her.
He gently told her that she was
    beautiful to Him,
That nothing had or ever would change
    that.
She listened as He told her He would
    heal her body and her soul,
Both inside and out.
That the blood of the cross would wash
    the shame away,
That all she had to do was hand it all
    over,
Every last drop of guilt, shame, anger
    even hate,
To be laid at the foot of the cross where
    Jesus laid down His life for her.

Then she will be proud to be a woman,
To see herself through His eyes,
To be comfortable that she is just as He
    created her,
And to finally stand tall with her head
    held high,
A princess of the King.

# The Shepherd

*After hearing the parable of the lost sheep I had a powerful picture of being that lost sheep, alone and afraid, trying to save myself in my own strength but failing and only then handing myself over to be saved, saved by my Shepherd, my true Father.*

The sheep felt safe and secure in their
    flock,
Sharing their warmth,
Protected by the Shepherd.
But out in the dark,
One little sheep was lost.
He didn't know how he had got onto the
    ledge of the cliff,
He didn't know how to escape the
    inevitable drop before him,
It seemed so impossible, so hopeless.

After spending a such long time
    searching for a way off the cliff,
The little sheep finally gave up,
Falling down with exhaustion.
Then he cried out desperately for the
    Shepherd as he knew now he was
    surely going to die.

But unbeknown to him the Shepherd
    heard his cry from afar that cold
    night.
The Shepherd got up and made His way
    through the darkness to find the lost
    sheep,

He climbed down the treacherous cliff to
    where the little sheep was trapped.
He then gently lifted the little weak
    sheep from the cliff ledge with His
    strong arms,
And cradled him securely against His
    heart,
Giving the shivering bundle His warmth
    on the way back to the flock.

Safe back with his family the little
    sheep slept peacefully,
Each time he woke up he looked over to
    the Shepherd by the flickering fire,
And he felt reassured and totally loved.
For he knew in his heart he would never
    be truly lost again.

*If a man has a hundred sheep, and one
of them has gone astray, does he not
leave the ninety-nine on the mountains
and go in search of the one that went
astray? And if he finds it, truly, I say to
you, he rejoices over it more than over the
ninety-nine that never went astray.*
*Matthew 18 v 12-13 ESV*

# A Walled City

*I had the amazing privilege to go to Hong Kong to teach. I stayed with a wonderful family and got to see and experience amazing things. But the one place I really wanted to visit was the site of the Walled City that Jackie Pullinger wrote about in her book 'Chasing the Dragon'. It was quite a journey and hard to get the taxi driver to understand where I wanted to go but I made it, and discovered myself in a beautiful park. The city was long gone but I found near the centre the 'Jackie Pullinger rock' and a plaque explaining her Christian missionary work in the Walled City. An amazing thing in a country where up to 80% claim no religion and Buddhism and Taoism are the main religions. There was her testimony in English and Mandarin for all to see, a simple woman going where no one dared to tread, touching the untouchable.*

> High walls surrounded the city,
> No one could see in,
> No one could see out.
> God was not welcome in this city,
> Desperate people refusing to hear His
>     voice.
>
> Until one day, one person had the
>     courage to go inside the walls,
> Had the courage to speak of a man
>     called Jesus,
> Changing lives through His story,
> The story of His life,
> The story of His death.
> How this death can bring new life.

Would those people ever have discovered
    their Saviour?
 If that one person had not come among
    them?
Treading where others dare not tread,
Seeking those who others thought
    beyond help.

She believed from her heart,
She saw with eyes of faith,
She trusted in God's love,
Walked through the city in His strength,
Shining with His living light,
Spreading the warmth of His true love.

Will I have the courage to step forward
    with eyes of faith?
To trust in His plan before I can see
    with my earthly eyes,
To tread where others will not tread?
To bring His word to those who have
    been abandoned,
Those without hope.
So they too can be reborn like I was,
Forgiven,
Loved,
Will I walk inside those walls?

# Ouch!

*On the team with MBM, I was having my morning shower in the usual miniscule shower cubicle in an on suite bathroom when somehow I managed to slip and fall, catching my toe. It was a funny shape and quickly swelled up, turning a dramatic shade of purple, I've done first aid for years so strapped it up to the toe next door which is the standard treatment for broken toes and proceeded to hobble about cross with myself for being so clumsy, but even then through that accident God spoke to me.*

"Ouch!" I exclaimed as I slipped and
    caught my toe,
It started to swell and bruise instantly,
Possibly broken.

Such a small bone and part of the
    essential process of walking that I do
    every day without thinking.

To treat a broken toe it's just strapped
    to the next one.
Using its neighbour for support.
A neighbour that's been next door all the
    time unnoticed but now vital,
So the foot can still function as one,
Part of a whole design, formed when I
    was created.

Amazing colours came out later,
But I could see that where that
  neighbouring toe had pressed there
  was no bruising.
It was protected.

Jesus is now my support.
When I am broken I can hold on to Him
  for dear life.
Strap myself to him in desperation with
  love and faith.

My life may have left me bruised and
  fractured,
But I know I can now always stand,
When I stand by His side
He will always protect me.
He will always hold me.
He will always love me.

With Jesus I am whole again just as my
  Father God created me.

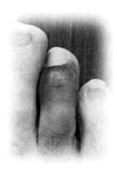

# Crashing Waves

*At Lee Abbey I was down in the bay on my own, spending some time reflecting, the tide was coming in and the waves were crashing spectacularly. I was so involved watching the waves I almost got caught out by the tide, it was only a wave suddenly splashing up over me that brought me out of my thoughts and made me realise. The bay has many rocks, steep cliffs and a beach area so the waves were very different all around, like the waves of life which change daily, hourly or even by the minute. God's love is not like that, it's a constant, it doesn't ebb and flow like the tide, He doesn't come and go. I may but He's always there.*

> The waves roar in,
> The waves roll out.
> They crash,
> They bang,
> They pound,
> Every day the same.
> The tide comes in,
> The tide goes out.
> Sometimes higher,
> Sometimes lower,
> Sometimes crashing wildly,
> Sometimes rolling gently.
> My love for God can seem high or low.
> Life crashes wildly around,
> And it can feel like maybe God has gone
>      out like the tide.
> Other day's life is rolling along gently,
> God seems right there beside me.

But in reality that's not true.
It's when life is crashing around,
When things are tough,
When I feel low,
That's when God is right there.
That's when He is shielding me from the
    fiercest waves.
That's when He holds me above the
    highest incoming tides.
That's when His love stops me from
    sinking to the bottom.
I just have to lift my eyes to Him,
To listen to His gentle voice,
To take hold of His loving Father hand.
For it's me that is sometimes distant,
Not God.
He's always there.
He's my Dad.

# Gods Plan

*God has a plan for each of us, we don't know it all, often He reveals it a bit at a time. I for one know I would have run a mile if I'd known what He'd got in store for me! Now I'm saved I have a future, a future that God planned for me before I was even born. I may not always understand where He is going with it so I must take that leap of faith and trust even if it's scary, as I know He's got it covered!*

Once I was lost but now I have been
    found.
I believed there was no plan,
I had no future,
I was at rock bottom,
And it would be where my life would
    end.
I was so, so lost.

When God first found me,
I tried to hide.
Scared of change,
Afraid of the unknown,
I did not understand.

I slowly learnt to trust in God,
To discover His unconditional love,
A love so different to any other love.
He started to show me His plan,
Only a small part at a time so I would
    not be afraid.

As He led me, I followed.
The unknown is still there,
But I am now walking forward,
Confident in the plan God has for me.
I was blind but now I see.

*"For I know the plans I have for you,"*
*declares the Lord, "plans for welfare and*
*not for evil, to give you a future and a*
*hope.  Then you will call upon me and*
*come and pray to me, and I will hear*
*you.  You will seek me and find me,*
*when you seek me with all your heart.  I*
*will be found by you," declares the Lord,*
*"and I will restore your fortunes and*
*gather you from all the nations and all*
*the places where I have driven you,"*
*declares the Lord, "and I will bring you*
*back to the place from which I sent you*
*into exile."*
*Jeremiah 29 v11-14 ESV*

# The Friars

*While Steve and I were going out we went for a walk around The Friars in Aylesford. It's a Catholic priory that is amazingly beautiful but stuck right by the M20 motorway. The sound of the traffic is always there in the background, all day and all night but it still feels a peaceful haven. It made me think how a haven can be anywhere, however busy I feel, however noisy life may be, God's peace is always in my heart.*

> It's amazingly beautiful and peaceful
> here.
> But all around I hear sound of the
> motorway,
> The rush of life,
> Everyone anxious to go from A to B in as
> little time as possible.
>
> As I hear busyness of life all around,
> I find I can still be calm,
> Find an oasis,
> Retreat with God.
> It doesn't matter where I am,
> There will always be a place that's still
> and quiet,
> A place where in my heart and soul I
> can rest, renew,
> And just be with You.

# The Cost

*Everyone is always talking about cost. How expensive everything is, prices that have gone up, our lives can revolve around money. It made me think of the real cost of me being here. The cost God paid to put His Son on the cross to die for me and for you. I will never truly understand the enormity of this cost, what He really gave, what Jesus willingly went through for me, but I do understand that it was from love, love for me.*

Cost seems so important.
Cost of living,
Cost of fuel,
Cost of food.

But how often do I think of the cost of my life?
How much it cost for Jesus to be on that cross,
His life for mine.

Was it worth it?
Can I make it worth it?
Can I live my life in honour of His?

I'll never really know or understand the cost,
But I know Jesus paid it for me through Gods
   love.

# There's Something in my Shoe....

*Rushing around Lee Abbey, I was so busy doing my sound job that I put up with a stone in my shoe all morning before I made time to sit down and finally take the shoe off and shake the stone out. Why didn't I do it sooner? Do I carry these small stones around in my heart, niggling away at my spirit? Do I need to stop, sit and shake them out, hand them over? Father please show me these stones in my heart and help me remove them forever.*

There's something in my shoe!
I noticed it at breakfast,
But was too busy to look.
I walked around for hours,
    uncomfortable,
The stone digging in my foot.

At coffee time I finally stopped, looked.
There seemed to be nothing there,
Was it empty?
I shook the shoe anyway,
And put it back on.
The stone had gone,
It did not hurt anymore,
Not niggling at me as I walked around.
All sorted.

Is there a small stone left in my heart?
Niggling away.
Am I rushing around,
Too busy with life,
To stop,
Shake myself of the small stone,
Stopping it hurting me as I walk
    through life.

What is it that's there Lord?
What's causing that pain?
"True complete forgiveness my child,"
He whispers,
"It's holding you back.
Hand it all over to me,
Shake off that final stone.
Only I will be left in your heart.
Only with My love can you walk at
    peace.

Stop,
Take out the stone,
And truly forgive."

# No Fear

*A small group from the Beacon Church was visiting China, staying in Dali. It was such a privilege to be there, but so different in so many ways. I realised when we were out that I wasn't afraid, even though so many things were so foreign to me. I've been abroad before and been scared, I was raped in a foreign country. So what was different now? I now know God. I'm protected always, He's always there beside me.*

The sun shines down from a clear blue sky,
The mountains standing over us,
Tall and magnificent,
Watching over the city, seeing everything.

As I explore, I feel the presence of God all
    around me,
The warmth of the sun on my skin reminds me
    of His love,
And I know then He is right there beside me.

And so I can stand tall with my head held high,
    feel no fear in a land I don't know.
The landscape may be different,
The language I can't understand,
But He remains constant,
With Him I am never a stranger,
Where I go He is there, has been there first.

If just my presence can show others of His
    presence,
Then I have a purpose,
A reason,
Part of His plan.

My love, from His love, is now our love.
We are all His people,
All the same.

# Boats

*Feeling unwell I stayed in the harbour while the others went to explore the temple. I sat and watched the tourist boats full of people, mainly Chinese, arriving and leaving. A steady, continuous procession. All that seemed to be left behind was their rubbish. Was that me? What would I leave behind from my trip to China? What would I take away with me?*

The boats come in,
The boats go out.
The people walk in,
The people walk out.
Into the villages,
The markets,
The temples.
Following, following.
What do they bring?
What will they leave?
Will anyone be any different?

As I pass through the village,
Walk down the street,
Sit in the courtyard of a house,
Will I be different?

Yes. I am.
Some of what I believe has been passed on,
Some of the love transferred.
From a smile,
A hello,
A handshake,
A gift.

For Jesus is within me,
Part of my body,
My soul
The source of my strength,
The giver of my love.
I leave Him wherever I go,
Where I tread He treads,
And through that I grow in my heart,
Strengthen my spirit,
I am changed.

Will anyone else be different?
I don't know.
But I do know that they will learn of Jesus,
And it's through knowing Jesus that they will
    change.
It's Him that changes lives, not me.

Boats come in,
Boats go out.
I walk in,
I walk out.
Things are now different,
Lives will be changed.

# The Journey

*The time had come, Steve had proposed to me and we were to be married. A new part of my life was about to begin, a life joined together by God with another living being, two spirits bought together by God's love. I wanted to read something at the blessing service and late one night these words came to me. The end of one journey and the start of a new one. So on the 10th of November 2012, Steve and I joined our hands in marriage.*

The path my life was following became darker
    and darker,
The road became blocked by huge boulders and
    rubble,
Piled so high not a single ray of light could get
    through.
There seemed no hope of moving the giant
    rocks,
Eventually no point in continuing to try.
My life was over.

But in the moment that I turned to God,
Things changed.
Chinks of light appeared,
For although I couldn't move the huge rocks,
He could.
Then others gradually joined Him and the
    barrier slowly came down.
Rubble was thrown away for ever.

And so life continued on,
My path was clearer.
I still climbed over boulders in the way.

I still tripped over rubble in my path.
But I could see the way ahead,
Light replacing dark.

A new branch in my path appeared one day.
I ignored it for a while,
Passing by on the same road as normal,
Trudging along.
One day something changed,
I felt different.
I took the new path even though I had no idea
    where it would lead and where I would go.

The new path lead to the man I now love,
The man I have married today.
Now I do not walk the path of life alone,
We move forward together.
The light seems so bright,
The way ahead so clear.
Steve, let me take your hand in mine,
Let us journey on together.
Let us follow our Father in love,
My love for you,
And our love for Him,
And I will live my life and walk on now with
    you.

# Here's My Heart

*Whilst on a church weekend with the MBM team I listened to Marilyn play her song 'Your love has melted my heart'. I'd heard it before but the time the line "here's my heart for eternity" struck deeply into my heart. I'd given my heart to people I trusted, for it to be taken and crushed. I'd trusted the wrong people, would I ever get it right? But trusting God is so different, He will never break that trust. Handing over my heart to Him truly was for all of this life and the next. Eternity.*

Here's my heart.
I have offered it many times before,
To others who have abused this precious gift.

Here's my heart.
It's been damaged so much,
Crushed by those who said they loved me.

Here's my heart.
Lord I give it to you,
I trust in you - there will be no better guardian
   of this fragile soul.

Here's my heart not for just now, tomorrow or
   the rest of my life but for eternity.
Here's my heart.

# Afterword

These poems (I call them poems just to have a label) are just me writing to, with and through God. It's how He speaks to me when I listen, what He says to me when something every day stands out and I stop to think why. Some are written in the night on my phone or iPod, others early morning, others when I'm out and about and the words come and I just have to stop and write them down, sometimes to others annoyance when I'm supposed to be doing something else! There's been at least one occasion when I've stopped putting the song words up on the screen in church because I've got carried away writing when I've been inspired....

I encourage you to write things down if you feel God speaking to you. It's a wonderful way to keep what Gods sharing with you, and also means you can share with others when the time is right like I have. It's been a real privilege to share many of my poems at events with Marilyn and Tracy, at church or at cell group. I have received feedback of the blessing that these words that God gave me have then given others. When Marilyn suddenly suggests I share a poem, I panic and think 'Oh no, what do I share?' I always find He guides me to the right one. Someone always finds me afterwards and speaks to me about what's troubling them or someone they know. A topic that's touched them, such as self-harm, depression, abuse or rape. I may then be able to pray with them or for them later. I never expected

I could do any of this, that God could ever use me, but I've learnt God can use any one of us. The weaker we are, the more He can use us, as we are not working in our own strength but in His.

When I look back over the last few years and see how far I have come; when I meet people that have not seen me since I was ill, unable to manage everyday life; its then I see the changes that have happened, the work that Gods done in me. The events that have happened, from abuse in my childhood to being raped whilst abroad in 2005, my return home, being unable to work, being so deeply depressed and suicidal, to almost dying through self-harm. These all brought me to a place where I would fling myself on God, totally surrender to Him. I wouldn't wish those things on anyone, but I wouldn't be the person I am today without that journey to rock bottom and back. I am here today because I found out God loved me, has always loved me, will always love me.

I am excited about the path ahead, Gods plan for Steve and I. We both still need healing, but we're on the journey together now, the three of us.

# Resources

## People and Organisations:

*MBM* – a dynamic itinerant ministry of music, teaching and prayer from Marilyn Baker and Tracy Williamson.
PO Box 393, Tonbridge, Kent TN9 9AY.
Tel: 01732 850855
http://www.mbm-ministries.org
Email: info@mbm-ministries.org
Prayer and information line: 0800 0193709

*LifeSIGNS* - a user-led voluntary organisation raising awareness about self-injury, with a mission to guide people who hurt themselves towards new ways of coping, when they're ready for the journey.
http://www.lifesigns.org.uk/
Email: info@lifesigns.org.uk

*The Beacon Church Herne Bay*
78 Sea Street, Herne Bay, Kent CT6 8QE
http://www.beaconhernebay.org.uk

*Torch Trust* - Christian resources and activities for blind and partially sighted people worldwide.
http://www.torchtrust.org/

*The Outlook Trust* – reaching older people with the good news of Jesus Christ.
http://www.outlook-trust.org.uk/

*Tony Horsfall, Charis Training* - Intimacy with God through the experience of grace
*http://www.charistraining.co.uk/*

*Jackie Pullinger, the St Stephens Society*
http://www.ststephenssociety.com/

*Akiane Kramarik* – artist and poet who began drawing at age 4 and had a spiritual transformation bringing her whole family to God. She completed her 5ft tall portrait of Jesus the Prince of Peace at age 8 which is featured in 'Heaven is for real' by Todd Burpo.
http://www.artakiane.com/

**Christian Centres:**

*Brunel Manor Christian Holiday and Conference Centre*
Teignmouth Road, Torquay, Devon, TQ1 4SF
Tel: 01803 329333
http://www.brunelmanor.com/contact
Email: info@brunelmanor.com

*Green Pastures* – A Christian retreat and renewal centre.
17 Burton Road, Poole, Dorset BH13 6DT
Tel: 01202 764776
http://www.greenpastures17.wordpress.com
Email: info@green-pastures.org

*Harnhill Centre of Christian Healing.*
The Harnhill Centre, Harnhill, Cirencester, Gloucestershire. GL7 5PX
Tel: 01285 850283
http://www.harnhillcentre.org.uk
Email: office@harnhillcentre.org.uk

*Haus Barnabas im Engel* -Christian guesthouse in the Black Forest for spiritual refreshment, encouragement and Gospel outreach.
Tel: 0049 7673 7760
Email: len.holder@haus-barnabas.com
Wiesentalstr 47, 79694 Utzenfeld, Germany.
http://www.haus-barnabas.com
http://haus-barnabas.blogspot.com

*Lee Abbey Christian Community*
Lynton, North Devon. EX35 6JJ
Tel: Freephone 0800 3891189 or 01598 752621
http://www.leeabbey.org.uk/devon/

*Offa House* - pray, learn and rest in God
Village Street, Offchurch, Warwickshire.
CV33 9AS
Tel: 01926 423309
http://offahouseretreat.co.uk/
Email: enquiries@offahouse.org

*Pilgrim Hall Conference Centre*
Easons Green, Uckfield, East Sussex. TN22 5RE
Tel: 01825 840295
http://www.pilgrimhall.com/home
Email: pilgrim@cwr.org.uk

*St Rhadagunds Christian Holiday and Conference Centre*
Undercliff Drive, St Lawrence, Ventnor, Isle of Wight, PO38 1XQ
Tel: 01983 852160
http://www.strhads.co.uk
E-mail: info@strhads.co.uk

## Other Places:

*Kowloon Walled City Park.*
Tung Tsing Road, Kowloon City, Kowloon, Hong Kong.
http://www.discoverhongkong.com/eng/see-do/culture-heritage/historical-sites/chinese/kowloon-walled-city-park.jsp

*The Friars*  encouraging an openness to God of anyone who comes.
Aylesford, Kent ME20 7BX
Tel: 01622 717272
http://www.thefriars.org.uk/contact.html

## Books:

*Flying Free With God*, Tracy Williamson (New Wine Press)

*Heaven Is For Real*, Todd Burpo with Llyn Vincent (Thomas Nelson)
http://heavenisforreal.net

*His Blood not Mine,* Hellen Jeans/Frost (A Passion for Learning)

*Recovery Devotional Bible, New International Version.* Ed. Verne Becker (Zondervan)

*The ESV Study Bible* (Crossway)

*The Everyday Life Bible (Amplified),* with commentary by Joyce Meyer (Faith Words)

*The Message Remix: the Bible in contemporary language,* Eugene Peterson (NavPress)

**Music:**

*Be Thou my Vision*. Traditional. (from the album *The Mandate: O Church Arise*), Stuart Townend (Kingsway).

*God Loves You (Outstanding)*, Steve Dunn and Hellen Jeans
http://stevangelical.wordpress.com/2011/10/22/new
-song-god-loves-you-outstanding/

*In Christ Alone* (from the album *There is a Hope*), Stuart Townend (Kingsway)
http://www.stuarttownend.co.uk

*Love is the Compass* (from the album *Home*), Nathan Tasker (Entertainment One Music)
https://nathantasker.com

*There is Power in the Name of Jesus* (from the album *All Heaven Declares*), Noel Richards (Kingsway)
http://www.noelrichards.com

*Your Love has Melted my Heart* (from the album *Overflow of Worship*), Marilyn Baker (Integrity Music)
http://www.mbm-ministries.org

Also by Hellen Frost

"Just picked up His Blood Not Mine again and have tears streaming" – L

"Your poetry is beautiful, moving and clear in its message, God is clearly using your ability to minister to others" – G

"I am not a lover of poetry and find "modern" poems the worst, but I did not go to bed last night until I had finished your book!!!! You have been very brave to bare your soul and I found them challenging, humbling, inspiring, provoking and encouraging" - D

Lightning Source UK Ltd.
Milton Keynes UK
UKOW04f2011200514

231988UK00001B/24/P